Fiddle Time Sprinters

Violin accompaniment book

Kathy and David Blackwell

Teacher's note

These duet parts are written to accompany the tunes in *Fiddle Time Sprinters*. They are an alternative to the piano accompaniments or CD, and are not designed to be used with those items.

We are grateful to Simon Stace for all his help in road-testing these duets.

Kathy and David Blackwell

MUSIC DEPARTMENT

OXFORD

UNIVERSITY PRESS

OXFORD
UNIVERSITY PRESS

Great Clarendon Street, Oxford OX2 6DP,
United Kingdom

Oxford University Press is a department of the University of Oxford.
It furthers the University's objective of excellence in research, scholarship,
and education by publishing worldwide. Oxford is a registered trade mark of
Oxford University Press in the UK and in certain other countries

ISBN 978-0-19-339857-3

Cover illustration by Martin Remphry

Music and text origination by Katie Johnston
Printed in Great Britain on acid-free paper by
Halstan & Co. Ltd, Amersham, Bucks.

Contents

1. Ready to rock

KB & DB

Determined

2. Clear skies

KB & DB

3. Ode to joy

(from Symphony No. 9)

Ludwig van Beethoven (1770–1827)

Joyfully

Also try this in 3rd position using the fingering given.

4. Song from the show

KB & DB

5. Starry night

KB & DB

6. Paris café

KB & DB

7. Gaudete!

Medieval carol

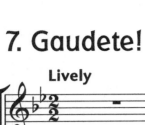

Lively

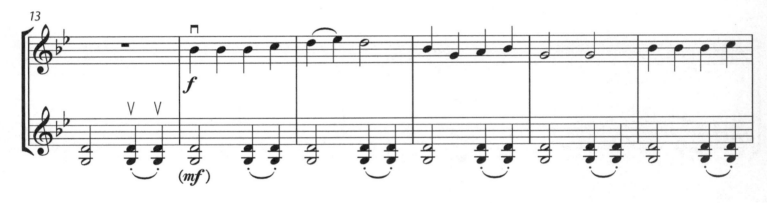

8. Jacob's dance

KB & DB

Rhythmic

mp

mp

Fine

cresc.

f

cresc.

f

mp

p

D.C. al Fine

mp

mf

p

mf

11

9. Sprint finish

KB & DB

accel. (ad lib.)

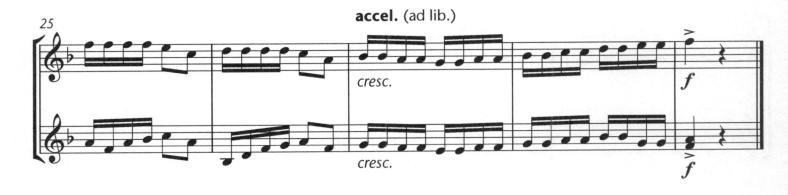

10. Bolero

Spanish trad.

11. William Tell

G. A. Rossini (1792–1868)

Allegro vivace

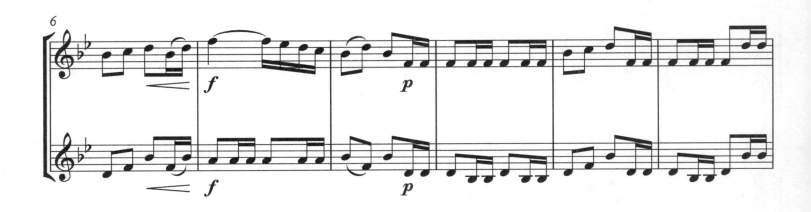

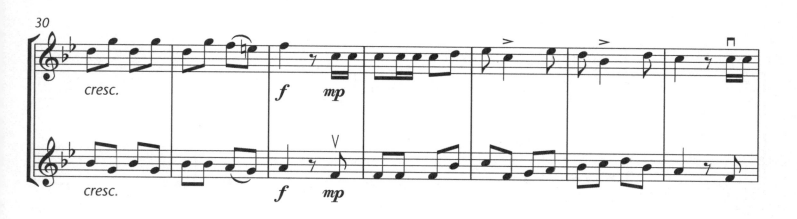

accel. (ad lib.)

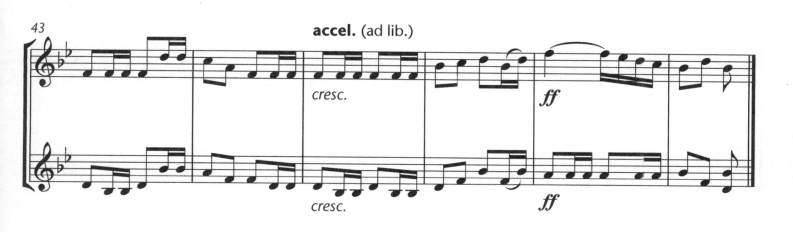

12. Country gardens

Lively

English Morris Dance tune

13. You and me

KB & DB

You and me!

14. The road to Donegal

KB & DB

15. Full circle

Gently

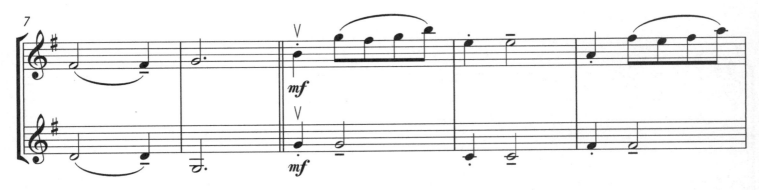

20

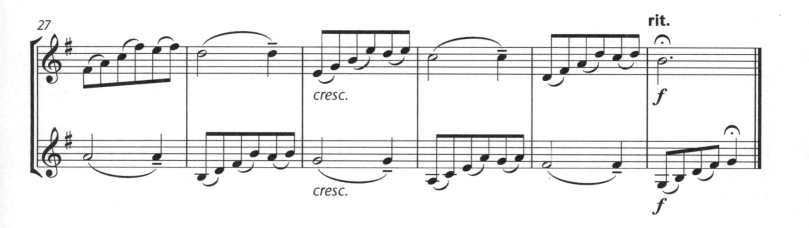

16. Thirsty work

KB & DB

Return to the chorus after each verse. The chorus and verse 1 can be played in semiquavers with spiccato bowing. The music is written out in full in the pupil's book.

17. Farewell to Skye

KB & DB

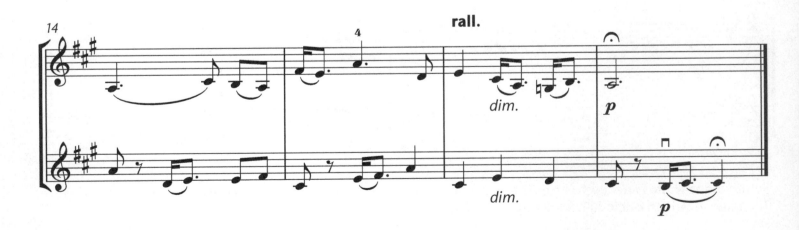

18. Lady Katherine's pavane

KB & DB

The pavane was a slow, stately court dance popular in the 16th and 17th centuries.

19. Dance of the Sugar Plum Fairy

(from the *Nutcracker* ballet)

P. I. Tchaikovsky (1840–93)

20. Allegro in A

G. P. Telemann (1681–1767)

Allegro

Try starting this piece with either a down or an up bow.

21. Still reeling

(based on *Blair Atholl,* trad. Scottish reel)

Add your own dynamics to this reel.

22. Mexican fiesta

KB & DB

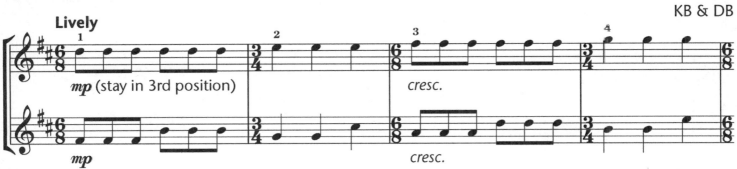

23. Show stopper

KB & DB

28

24. Spy movie

KB & DB

25. Largo

(from the *New World* Symphony)

Antonín Dvořák (1841–1904)

26. Hornpipe

(from the *Water Music*)

G. F. Handel (1685–1759)

Allegro moderato

33

27. Hungarian folk dance

KB & DB

(2nd time **accelerando**)

28. Wild West

KB & DB

Hoe-down

29. Midnight song

KB & DB

Peaceful

30. Wade in the water

Spiritual

Insistent

31. Dominant gene

KB & DB

32. Chromatic cats

KB & DB

Creeping

33. Show off!

KB & DB

34. Little lamb

Spiritual

35. Habanera

(from *Carmen*)

Georges Bizet (1838–75)

Allegretto quasi Andantino

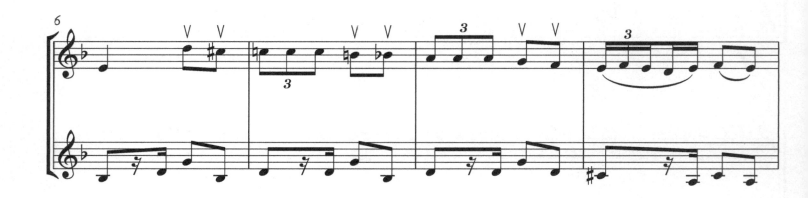

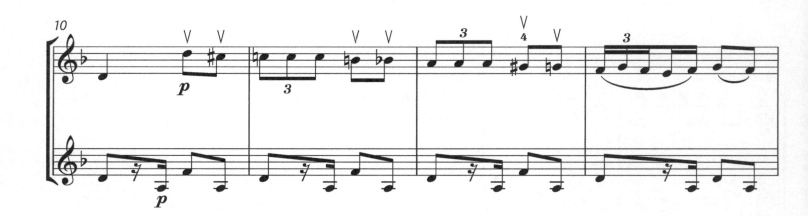

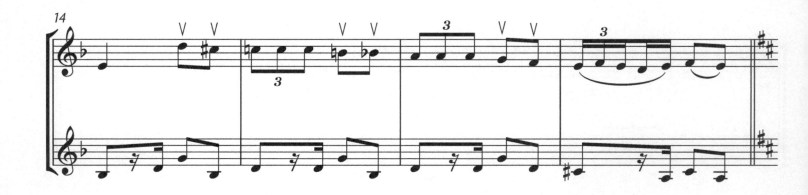

Round up

Play these rounds or canons in 2 or more parts, entering at *.

36. Alleluia

William Boyce (1711–79)

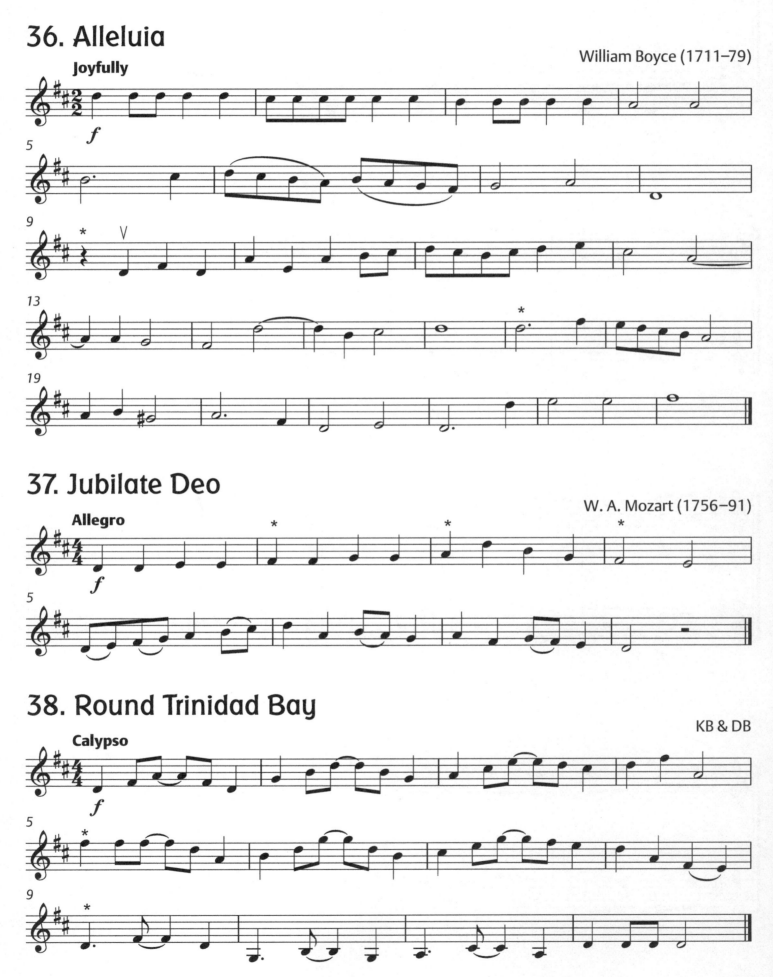

37. Jubilate Deo

W. A. Mozart (1756–91)

38. Round Trinidad Bay

KB & DB